MW01517593

SUCCESSFUL SELF-
PUBLISHING

(non-fiction)

HOW TO WRITE A BOOK
IN 30 DAYS (OR LESS)

- a 7-step guide to writing a good book fast -

Kevin Albert

You don't have to be great to start,
but you have to start to be great.

—ZIG ZIGLAR

CONTENTS

Introduction

I remember one day, when I was seven or eight, my teacher gave me a note to give to my mother. The note asked my mother for a meeting so that they could talk about me and my academic performance (back in the days before teacher-parent WhatsApp groups). I don't remember exactly whether the meeting went well or not, but what I do remember is what my mother said when she got home: "Kevin, your teacher says you're a smart kid, but that she thinks you're writing badly on purpose to get her attention."

Sadly, I wasn't writing badly on purpose or to get attention; I simply wasn't very good at it, and my handwriting didn't help - and it still doesn't!

To this day, I'm always being told I "write like a doctor".

Fear of writing is something that stayed with me right through my college years. My grades always got lowered in every test, either because I couldn't express myself well or because they couldn't read my handwriting. Unlike the rest of my classmates, I would cross my fingers for a quiz-type test, because I couldn't just write my way out of it.

Fortunately, my adventurous streak has always been stronger than my fears, and around 2012, I had the brainwave of turning a piece of college work I was doing for my MBA[1] into a book.

A book! Me?! What the hell was I thinking?

---

[1] Master of Business Administration

I could have spent the weekend cramming with three classmates and got an outstanding grade for that piece of work - but I decided to go it alone. I ended up spending **four years** on it.

I can promise you that the process wasn't easy; I came close to throwing in the towel on several occasions. Four years is a long time. Fortunately, I had a secret weapon: sheer stubbornness. When I set my mind to something, sooner or later, I do it. Armed with this tenacity that's always been a part of me, I overcame every obstacle that sprang up in my path, and - swearing to myself that I would never put myself through such an ordeal again - I found the way to finish my first book.

In mid-2016, everything was finally complete, and the long-awaited "publish on Amazon" button was finally ready for me to click.

Click!

So, what the hell happened after that moment that made me go from swearing I would never write another book, to making it my life's work? And more importantly, how did I go from spending four years writing a book to finishing one in under 30 days?

That's exactly what the book you're holding will tell you.

1. I'm going to show you **the amazing things that await you after you publish your book** (things I could scarcely have imagined), so that you don't have to depend on pig-headedness, like I did.

2. I'm going to **teach you the exact system that enabled me to go from writing a book in four years to doing it in 30 days or less**, saving you years of learning and of trial and error.

And, best of all, you don't need:

- To be a great writer.
- To have a degree.
- To be a bookworm.
- To have a lot of free time.
- To be an expert in your field.
- ...

All you need is something you want to tell the world. My mission is to show you how to do it.

Shall we get started?

Why write a book?

I bet, since you're reading this book, you think you already have this point covered and you can skip this chapter. Don't make that mistake; without a doubt, this is the most important chapter in the whole book.

Having a **just because** and having a **sufficiently important reason** can mean the difference between writing your book in 30 days, taking a really long time (like I did), or - most commonly - never finishing or even starting it.

Of course, not all books can be written in the same space of time; some good books are so specific and short that they can be written in one day (I know of more than one such book), while others are so long or require so much prior research that they can take several months. But it should never take **years**!

As I said, my big "mistake" - which made my first book _Branding Secrets_[2] take **much longer than it should have** to see the light of day - was not having a **sufficiently important** reason for it.

Branding Secrets began as a piece of work for a Corporate Image and Identity module on my Master's in Business Administration at college. Of course, within a traditional education system, your motive is clear: **passing**. No one was going to give me a prize for writing a book that was revolutionary in the branding world or one with the potential to change thousands or millions of

---

[2] soykevinalbert.com/branding-secrets

people's lives. The only thing that mattered was that my teacher liked it, so that I could get a good grade. And I did. With only twenty written pages, my work was the only one to pass with honors, out of over forty students on that MBA course.

But once I had passed, what was my motive for continuing to write? As I'm sure you've figured out, I had none. So how did I manage to finish my book? That's easy: through willpower. The only source of energy I had at my disposal when it came to finishing my book was pure and simple pig-headedness. I can't think of any better recipe for ensuring a project's failure. Despite this, and against all odds, I managed to finish and publish my book - albeit four years later.

How much easier and faster would it have been to write if I had known what awaited me when it was finished? How long would I have taken to finish it had I known **the power a book has to change your life**?

What can a book do for you?

In a word: EVERYTHING.

Think I'm exaggerating? Or that that's just my opinion? Nope. **A book can fulfil your needs on every single level.**

But don't just take my word for it; I can prove it scientifically, using Maslow's hierarchy.

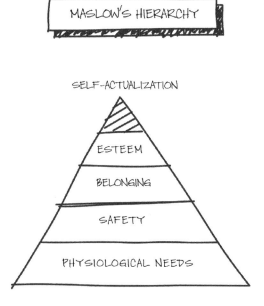

Maslow's hierarchy of needs is a motivational theory that aims to explain what drives our behavior by showing human needs ranked on a five-level pyramid.

This theory posits that as our more basic needs are fulfilled (the lower levels of the pyramid), humans develop more elevated needs and wants (the higher levels). However, usually, a book will fulfil the writer's needs in reverse order - that is, from top to bottom. Let's take a look.

1. The need for self-actualization.

Every writer I have spoken to, and every writer I've read about, agrees that finishing a book and holding the first hard copy of it in your hands produces a sensation of accomplishment and self-actualization that is hard to beat. It's not surprising, considering you have just achieved a feat that most people dream of but only 1%

actually do. Don't deny yourself this extraordinary feeling of self-actualization.

2. Esteem needs.

Have you ever wondered why we need to be considered experts on certain topics? To have a college degree, maybe? Or two? Three? A masters? A blog? A YouTube channel? A gazillion Instagram followers?

Other than having a doctorate or being on a TV show, I can't think of a better way to achieve immediate recognition than by writing a book. But, unlike the doctorate, it won't take half your life to finish - especially if you follow the tips in this book.

3. Belonging needs.

Almost parallel to our need for esteem comes the need for belonging. Like it or not, writing a book will automatically make you a member of the select club of super-writers: one that, as I mentioned, only 1% of people are invited to join.

You know how sharing political views, a nationality or a football team brings people together? Well, wait till you experience the camaraderie produced by talking to other people who have been through the painstaking, solitary process of becoming a writer. It's like spending months lost in a country where you don't know anyone, and suddenly bumping into your oldest friend.

I can promise you that, in less than a year and requiring no further effort on your part, several very interesting people will have joined your circle of friends: people who, just like you, wrote a book.

4. Safety needs.

Do you think having a salaried job provides security? Wait till you experience the peace of mind of having a **recurring passive income**. It's like getting your pension *now,* but without the uncertainty. In case you didn't know, experts agree that the days of pensions as we know them are numbered.

But don't panic; that's why you're here. You can tailor your own retirement plan - and not only that, but you can create as many **retirement books** or plans as you want.

If you're a clued-up person, then it's a very good idea for your retirement to depend on you and not on a tight-fisted, incompetent government.

5. Physiological needs.

Obviously, both the passive and non-passive (services, talks, and so on) incomes from your book will enable you to put food on the table and sleep easy at night: two very important basic physiological needs.

But there is a third need that writing a book can fulfil, and it's not such an obvious one: the need for reproduction.

Because whether you like it or not, writing a book will turn you into a much more interesting and attractive person. And in a society that claims to be sapiosexual[3], I think this is a much better alternative to salsa classes when it comes to finding a partner.

Okay, so now we've scientifically corroborated the fact that **a book has the power to fulfil all your needs**. But no matter how impressive this headline seems, or how nice it is to hold the benefits of a book up alongside the pyramid of human needs, this may not be **enough motivation for you to ensure you both**

---

[3] By definition, a sapiosexual is someone who finds intelligence sexually attractive or arousing.

start *and finish* your book, since you probably already had most of these needs covered.

So, if you want to find a source of motivation strong enough that it doesn't run out halfway through, you're going to need to be a lot more practical and pragmatic.

Why write a book?

There are as many reasons to as there are stars, so I'm just going to focus on what I think are **the 7 best reasons to write a book**:

1. Live without having to work.

Most of us spend our lives waiting for five o'clock so we can go home, waiting for Friday to start the weekend, waiting for August to go on vacation, waiting to turn sixty-seven so we can finally **retire and be free to do what we want**.

But be careful. Many of us may not make it to sixty-seven, or life expectancy may increase to the point that we're made to work five or ten years longer, or pensions may run out, or we may not have the good health to enjoy retirement, and so on. So why risk it? Why wait?

It's true that earning millions of dollars from a first book is a rare occurrence, and it depends on having - among other factors - exceptional talent and a considerable amount of luck.

But **earning a thousand dollars a month through passive income from your book requires nothing more than a good strategy**.

Of course, your first book might earn you a little (or a lot) more than that (although I can't guarantee it). You may also make less, or need twice or three times as much in order to retire the way that you want. No problem. All you have to do is write another book or two...or as many as you want!

2. Fire your boss.

Unlike the reason given above, this one isn't about no longer working, but no longer working for your dick of a boss - a highly motivational idea. In this case, your book wouldn't be your (main) source of income, but **the way you generate your income**.

Let's look at an extreme example. Let's say you decide to give your book away for free (I don't recommend it at first). Your income from sales of your book would be zero, but you would start to reach more people than if you were charging for it. These people would consider you an expert, and - if you did your homework - you'll become their preferred option when they need to hire an expert in the subject of your book.

Your book can be the best ad campaign for selling your products or services.

This is the most common situation. Even if you wrote a mediocre book and have no strategy, offers will start to pour in. The lives of many non-fiction writers change for the better, whether they planned it or not.

Bear in mind that being an "expert" is not an absolute. If you know just a little more than someone else on a given topic, to them, you are an expert.

Anyway, in your case - starting with a clear reason in mind for tailoring the best strategy for your specific situation - your life will not only change for the better, it will change in precisely the direction that you choose.

If you've just been cruising along, dictated by the circumstances and events of your day-to-day life, this could be a good moment to set a course you can sail toward.

Writing a book is a great opportunity to take the helm in your life.

3. Get your dream job.

In my dreams, I don't work, but I understand that many people need the approval and recognition that you can only get from X person or company considering them good enough to work for them. If this sounds like you, writing a book will multiply by one hundred (I made this statistic up, but I don't think I'm too far off) your chances of being the chosen candidate, even without an open selection process!

Yes, this means that if you write a book bearing in mind your aim to get a particular job, you can more or less publish it and then sit back and wait for that call - the company, and not you, will be able to decide you are the right person for the job. Have *your* conditions ready.

It might sound like I'm bragging, but it's really just common sense. If you write a book on a given subject, your target market is probably going to include the person hiring at the company (or company type) where you want to work. And if you write the book demonstrating you're an expert in the topic and dropping in the idea you're open to job offers (for example, in your LinkedIn profile), particularly that you're open to a challenge, which employers love, you have a great edge over people who may even be far more qualified than you.

A book is the best way for an "expert" to show off.

This doesn't mean that, if you're trying to find work, you can forget about actively looking for a job. All I want to do is highlight the competitive advantage a book can give you when it comes to being the winning candidate.

Now, all you have to do is plan out a good strategy to ensure your book ends up in the right hands.

4. Forget about your mortgage.

Maybe you're not looking to stop working; maybe your boss is great and you've already found your dream job. Maybe you already think your life is perfect just the way it is. But wouldn't it be a little more perfect if you could forget about your mortgage, change your car every two years instead of every twenty, or go on vacation more often to more exotic places?

It's up to you. Which expense sucks away a little of your happiness every month? What desire have you been postponing for years, waiting for a pay rise or a little lottery win?

The recurrent income from your book will enable you to improve your quality of life by several degrees. Bear in mind that as soon as you publish your book on Amazon (or anywhere else), you will receive a check or deposit every month from book sales - your royalties - without you having to lift a finger, and for the rest of your life[4]. Amazon will take care of absolutely everything, so all you will have to do is decide what to use your new "pay rise" for.

5. Spend your life traveling.

The vast majority of people, when you ask them what they would do if they won the lottery, don't miss a beat before replying "travel", "travel more", or "travel the world". Personally, I think this answer is just a knee-jerk reaction that reveals that that person has never truly stopped to think what they would really do if money were

---

[4] No one knows if Amazon will be around forever, or if they will change their conditions without prior notice. Don't worry - there are a lot of ways to get by without Amazon. For the moment, your only goal - and the aim of this book - is to start and finish your book.

no object. Even my mother, who can't be out of the house for more than a few hours, gives the same answer. I don't know about that...

In any case, whether this is really your dream or you just want to try it for a while, writing a book can give you this power, too. You also have several options to see which best suits you and your specific situation:

a) Spend your life traveling without working:

- Traveling thanks to the passive income generated by your book or books.

b) Spend your life traveling while working:

- Traveling thanks to the services you sell via your book. Your services should be available online, not just face-to-face.

- Traveling thanks to the passive income generated by your book while you continue to create new books. If you can only offer your services face-to-face, you can make writing books your new job.

The best thing about this is that, if you really want, you can start virtually straight away. For example, if you don't mind starting out in, let's say, Thailand, all you need is around three hundred and fifty dollars a month in income - passive or otherwise - which is not too difficult to achieve.

You might fall in love with the country and decide to stay there forever, never needing to work again. You might get bitten by the travel bug and want to visit other countries (or improve your quality of life in the one you're in). Given that you will have a lot of free time, why not write another book? You could even write about your experience. Picture it: *How I Retired and Moved to Thailand After Writing my First Book.*

When you publish your new manuscript, you'll have double the passive income, if not more, since you will have learned a lot since you published your first.

Now that you've decided to double your pay, maybe you'll want to try living in Bali. I've heard it's amazing, and with a thousand dollars a month you can live like a king, all inclusive. And what about publishing another book after that? Where do you want to move to next? Sounds good, huh? Best of all, this is **more than feasible**.

Are you getting ready to throw yourself into this yet?

6. Be immortal.

I've always been fascinated by the concept of immortality. I was a big fan of the *Highlander* saga as a child, and nowadays it's *Black Mirror* episodes centered around the idea that captivate me. I even follow news on new technological and scientific discoveries that suggest that, in a not-so-distant future, we will be able to live forever. But until that happens (if it ever does), the best way of guaranteeing your immortality is to leave behind a legacy.

I'm sure you've heard the expression: "every man should plant a tree, have a child, and **write a book**." All three of these ideas revolve around leaving a legacy and becoming immortal.

They say that you only truly die when no one remembers you any more. Writing a book is a fantastic way to keep your memory alive forever, and - contrary to what I believed when I was little - it's much easier, faster and less effort than having a child :)

7. Change the world.

I decided to leave this reason for last, because it's "my" reason. This is my greatest source of energy, my raison d'être while writing these words.

Personality, I think you can measure a person's worth or greatness by the number of lives they touch or enrich. As a serial entrepreneur, every one of my many projects is conceived as a way to cover a need that people find unfulfilled.

The problem is that when your direct intervention is needed in order to change people's lives, your potential to change the world radically decreases. How many people can you offer your services to in one year? Ten? Fifty? A thousand?

Even in the highly unlikely event that you can touch a thousand people's lives in a year, it's still an insignificant number. Your potential is tremendously limited because you need to dedicate x minutes or hours to each person in order to bring about significant change in their lives; there are only twenty-four hours in a day, and you can't be in two places at once.

Or can you?

A book will enable you to "be in two places at once", exponentially increasing your ability to reach and touch the lives of millions of people anywhere around the world, with a product that's accessible on any size budget.

Do you have an important message to share? Something you believe we should all know? or do you "simply" know how to make the best vegan burgers in the entire world or know a trick for traveling on a shoestring?

Without a doubt, there are dozens of ways to expand your message and your knowledge beyond one-on-one: conferences, a blog, a YouTube channel, and more, and they are all perfectly valid. Even so, my advice is still to start with a book. This will open numerous doors for you, and your opportunities to keep spreading your message will increase - but first, you need to take that first step.

Are you ready to begin your first book?

Excuses and writers' block: How to overcome them

Now you're clear on your reason for doing this, write it down. Congratulations! You have just completed the most important step in the journey of every successful writer.

If your chosen reason is important enough, nothing can stand in the way of you finishing your book.

But let's imagine you only chose a good reason. Good reasons are all well and good, and they get you far out in front of people who just started writing one day because they suddenly felt like it, but they're not foolproof.

What's the difference between a good reason, and a sufficiently important one? Let's take a look at an example:

- **A good reason**: I would *like* to write a book so I can get a better job and feel more accomplished.
- **A sufficiently important reason**: I *have* to write a book if I want to safeguard my children's future[5].

Does this mean that if you only have a *good* reason, you will never finish your book? No - it just means that you're going to need to brace yourself for the dreaded **writers' block.** And believe me, it will hit you.

---

[5] This is the real reason of a client and friend of mine, who puts a monthly portion of the proceeds from his book away in Indexa Capital (soykevinalbert.com/indexa). We calculated that, by the time his son is 22, the fund will be worth somewhere between $50,000 and $120,000.

If your reason is not important enough, your excuses will be.

Have you ever signed up for the gym totally convinced that this time, you'll get your dream body or shift those few extra pounds? What happened to your motivation after a few short weeks? Your *one-time* energy - in other words, your *good* reason - clashed with your *long-lasting* excuses: "I don't think I'll go today; it's raining", "I had a shitty day today and I deserve a rest", "I had an awesome day today and I want to celebrate it", and so on.

As a personal trainer, one of the most important parts of my job is preparing my clients for these kinds of excuses, because they will crop up sooner or later. If you wait for them to happen before doing anything about them, it will be too late.

Just like in fitness, excuses or writers' block always consist of the same thing - but don't worry, I have good news. There is an easy solution for them.

The 5 most common excuses writers make.

1. A book has to be perfect.

Without a doubt, this is my main block. I've always been a real perfectionist, so my projects have taken much longer than they should have. Of course, writing my first book was going to involve this, too.

I'm normally a perfectionist, even with the small tasks that have no real impact on my life, so imagine the unnecessary and inhuman effort I made when writing *Branding Secrets*. Of course, it was my first book and - I believed at the time, my last - and I thought it was going to be my legacy and show how good or mediocre I was, that people were going to judge me by it, and that once it had been published I could no longer change it.

My head was swimming with these thoughts and many others, and the same happens to lots of new writers. Well, let me tell you two things: firstly, most of them aren't true, and secondly (and more importantly) the success of a non-fiction book doesn't lie in how well-written it is, but in whether or not it delivers what it promises.

Unlike with fiction books, readers are not merely looking to be entertained or enjoy the pleasure of reading. When we buy a non-fiction book, we're looking to learn something, resolve a specific problem, acquire a new skill, and so on.

As such, even if your book isn't perfect - even if it's a total disaster in terms of spelling, grammar and structure - **if a reader finishes**

your book feeling that they found what they were looking for, you will have a satisfied reader.

Does this mean I give you my blessing to write a pile of trash? Of course not! All I'm saying is that you should focus on fulfilling your promise, and this will help you overcome "analysis paralysis" or "perfectionists' block". There will be time to worry about form later.

Still unsure what I mean? Here are a few more tips to help you get past the blockage:

- What might be just a rough draft for you could be a finished book for someone else.
- Your book will go through at least one meticulous editing process before being published, so relax.
- When someone reads your book on Kindle, they have the option to let you know automatically if they come across an error; it's kind of like having a whole team of

editors working for you. Not half bad, huh? But be careful - don't rely exclusively on readers.

- **On-demand printing from Amazon enables you to keep making corrections and improvements FOREVER**. Missed out an apostrophe? Had a reader point out a typo? Want to add additional information? No problem: you can edit the file, re-upload it and you're good to go. This is the beauty of this type of printing, among many other advantages.

Remember: perfect is the enemy of good.

2. You have to be an expert to write a book.

As we've already seen, you DON'T need to be an expert to write a book. You don't need a doctorate or to have read every single book, article and publication on a given topic. But...

Writing a book will turn you into an expert.

There's no better way to become an expert at something than to try and teach that something to someone else.

I have so many crazy examples of people I know doing this that I could write a whole book on them alone. I myself am an example of it; when I started writing *Branding Secrets*, I had a lot of experience and some very interesting things to say on the subject, but I was just a student back then and no one would have thought to ask me about branding. Now, I'm a major expert in low cost branding and I get offers from businesspeople and entrepreneurs from all over the world to help them with their brands, and they pay me very well for it (up to **a hundred times more** than in my old job working for other people). But, as I say, I did already know a lot about the topic. I was already an expert. My book really helped to give me more reach and visibility. So, to help you overcome your block, I'm going to tell you about one of those crazy examples I mentioned: one where the egg came before the chicken (or was it the other way around?). In other words, the book preceded the expert:

After spending two years working as a physiotherapist, traveling the world aboard the biggest cruise ship from the *Royal Caribbean*, I decided to make the most of the sales expertise I had acquired over the course of all those months[6]. So, on my return to Spain, I applied to work as a salesman; it was the only work where I could make a living close to what I had been earning on the boat.

For the next two years, I ascended the ranks of a company in the water treatment field, mainly

---

[6] In addition to my Physiotherapy qualifications, to work for many cruise companies you needed to spend several months at the company's Steiner facilities in the UK, where you think they're going to be teaching you new treatment techniques when what they're really doing is teaching you how to sell ice to an eskimo.

selling domestic osmosis purification systems. These kinds of companies generally had their employees work independently, with income coming from sales commissions. This way, the more salespeople they had knocking on doors, the better. It meant more opportunities to get sales. Anyone was welcome; you would have had to be truly awful for the company to fire you, since it didn't cost them anything to keep you on.

Well, I met someone who was *that* awful. The guy had presented himself as a sales whiz, but he couldn't sell anything. He was claiming unemployment, though, so he hung onto the job. Finally, the company had to fire him; he was demotivating all the new salespeople. Imagine the drama.

Then - out of luck rather than strategy - this guy decided to take advantage of his last few months on unemployment to write a book. And what did he write about? Sales! Imagine! And how do I know this? Because a colleague of mine who carried on working for the company after I left called me a few years later and told me the following story:

The company had scheduled a training trip to Barcelona for all the managers. There, they would spend two days attending a series of conferences on sales techniques delivered by the biggest sales experts in the world.

Guess who one of those speakers was?

The really awful guy! And he had the balls to tell them all that he had been kicked out of his job for not making sales, and that he had gone on to write a book and now spent his days giving talks and advising salespeople for big companies.

My friend told me: "Dude, after the conference I went over to talk to him and found out he earned more for that 45-minute talk than what I earn in a good sales month. And he delivers two to five conferences a month!"

Like I said, it was really crazy. This is a clear example of a snake oil salesman, which I talk about a lot in *Branding Secrets*.

I'm not using this example to encourage you to become a snake oil salesman by writing a book as a starting point. I just want to show you that not only can you write without considering yourself an expert, but **you can actually succeed with your book**. Let go of your fears and do it!

3. I'm not a writer (or I don't like to write, or I don't know how).

When I was at school, if someone had told me I would one day write a book, become an international bestselling author and end up helping people from all over the world to write their own books *and live off them*, I would have thought they were insane.

As I explained, expressive capabilities were never my strong point, as well as my spelling difficulties and my doctor's handwriting. Fortunately for me (and for you), these days, you DON'T need to be a great writer to be able to make a living from your books. **All you need is a message to spread**: knowledge or experience that can help other people.

If - like me - you don't like writing or you're not good at it, leave the technical side to your editor (we'll look at this later on). **You just focus on writing a draft of what you actually want to say**. You can also record yourself speaking if you prefer, and then have someone else transcribe it or use a free IT program to do it.

You can even go a step further. It's no secret that many writers, once they achieve fame with one of their books, start using the services of a ghostwriter. If you're not familiar with the term, a ghostwriter is simply a professional author hired to write on someone else's behalf to be published under that person's name.

Until recently, this was an elitist service that was hard to access - but today, you can find it with a simple Google search. Not only can you find freelance ghostwriters - there are also real platforms full of professional authors ready to write your book for you for just a few cents per word. Do you really think those politicians and celebrities could write a six-hundred-word book?

Every time the thought enters your mind that you can't write a book, **remember that Paris Hilton wrote a New York Times Bestseller.**

4. The myth of the printed book.

When you start to seriously consider writing a book, one of the first fears you have is often "a book should be at least X pages long", "I don't have that much to say", "I need to gather more material in order to write a decent book", and so on.

I was in the same boat myself. When I started writing my first book, I was convinced I didn't have that much to say and that I would only end up writing a few pages. This only got worse when I found out that Amazon - the platform I had chosen to self-publish on - required at least a hundred pages in order to be hardback. How could I publish a book that wasn't in hardback? It would be little more than a pamphlet!

Let me tell you something that will quickly help you past this stumbling block.

Firstly:

Though you may feel you don't have much to say, once you start writing, you'll see that your real problem is being able to stop: knowing what to exclude from your book so that it's not too long and boring.

If, for some reason, this doesn't happen, and your book ends up rather thin (though I really doubt it), you have several tricks at your disposal:

- Make the font a little bigger.
- Choose a font that naturally takes up more space.
- Increase your line or paragraph spacing.
- Select a smaller book format - Amazon (KPD) offers a wide range of sizes.
- Include photos, drawings and diagrams, but make sure they add value and are properly integrated.

You'll see it's easy to reach a hundred pages and get your hardback by following these simple tips - although, as I said, this probably won't be necessary. I tend to write quite concisely, so I calculated that by this point in this book, I would have written around ten pages. I haven't done my clean-up yet, but I'm at over fifty. Trust me when I say that you will be more likely to go on for too long than to struggle to write enough.

And secondly:

Not only is it hard for writers to find the time to write, it's also getting harder for readers to find the time to sit down and read. That's why short books are becoming more popular - so much so that Amazon has created a special category for them, known as "short reads". These titles take between eleven minutes and two hours to read.

Finally, let me share with you some interesting facts that will help you overcome your fear of writing a book that's "too short":

- For non-fiction books, people prefer a total of somewhere between ten thousand and twenty thousand words.
- Readers are far more likely to finish a short book than a longer one. People want books that focus on a specific issue rather than huge tomes that take on every single aspect of a topic.
- It's easier to market several shorter books than one long one.
- Having several books in an Amazon category rather than a single long book will help you to dominate that category.

5. I don't have time.

I've left this excuse till last because I hear it the most often: "I have no time", or "writing a book is too much work".

Firstly, with the right system in place, writing a book is not much work, so it doesn't matter if you're short on time.

I myself **wrote and published this and another four books in under three months** while also launching my first crowdfunding campaign, managing the manufacture of XQUAT® (the world's first portable professional gym), advising two large companies on their purchase funnel and three clients on their book launches, starting out in long-term stock market investment and finishing my *Coaching Behaviour Change* certification. Phew! And, of course, I still had time for Netflix, my weekly workout, meditating at least three times a week, reading, going out for drinks, and so on.

In this book, I'm going to show you how you can finish yours in just 30 days by dedicating around an hour a day to it, even if - like me - you're on a tight schedule.

As you can see, you don't need a Nobel Prize for Literature or all the free time in the world to write a book. All you need is to set aside an hour a day to "do your homework". In other words: **all you need to write a book is a little discipline**.

In any case, if you want to write a book but you know perseverance isn't your strong point, I would love to help you out personally, and charge dearly. I've helped so many people get in shape (as a personal trainer) or finish their books simply by being there to remind them that it's time to write or to go for a run. It's an expensive alarm, but a highly effective one. If you need that, call me! ;)

What to write: how to find the perfect idea for your book

One of the things I hear most, from friends and acquaintances as well as from clients, is: "I'd love to write a book, but I don't know what to write it about."

Whether this is you or, on the contrary, you have dozens of ideas and just don't know which one to start with, you should find this chapter tremendously useful. Even if you're clear on what book you want to write (which is a great start), doing the exercise I'm about to suggest might help you find a good focus for starting to write.

4 strategies for finding the perfect idea for your book

1. What things do people tend to ask you?

(Knowledge)

Obviously, if you're a lawyer, doctor, physiotherapist, or whatever else, people around you probably constantly bombard you with questions about your profession - but you don't need a college degree. I'm sure that my neighbor, who started going to the gym less than six months ago and has pumped his body full of more chemicals than a racehorse, gets asked much more than me - with my college education in health and sport and over twenty years of working out under my belt - how to get biceps bigger than your head or the best ab exercises.

I'm sure that you're an "expert" at something, too. Remember: just knowing a little more than someone else about a topic makes you an expert in that person's eyes.

Think about it: what do people tend to ask you about? Do you make a mean lasagne and everyone wants the recipe for it? Have you started a blog or website? Did you lose thirty pounds through a good diet and even better sex? Do you know how to get free stuff through Amazon (my cousin has a real gift for it)?

It doesn't matter how simple it seems or how easily you can find information by searching online. If you can save people's time by expressing your knowledge in a coherent, organized manner, lots of people will be prepared to pay for it.

2. Obstacles and challenges you've faced.

(Experiences)

This type of knowledge and experience is highly valued. Nothing sells better than "I hit rock bottom and still came out on top"-type stories. It's a resource often used in persuasive writing and copywriting and known as "hero's journey", and it lends authority and credibility that can turn an ordinary book into a real bestseller.

Ask yourself what difficult situations you've been in over the course of your life. Did you overcome a domestic violence situation? Did you beat alcohol or drug addiction? Have you had cancer? Maybe just reading these questions has your hair standing on end (especially if it's a subject close to home for you). Imagine the power these kinds of books can possess.

But there's no need to be dramatic about it. I wrote this book during the 2020 state of emergency during which we had to isolate in our houses for over thirty days. If you went through lockdown too, I'm sure you have a challenge to write about.

How I went through self-isolation...

- ...and used the time to write a book?
- ...without going stir crazy?
- ...and got in shape?
- ...without getting a divorce?
- Etc.

3. The things you like.

(Interests)

Want to know the easiest way to find a topic for your book? Take a look at:

- The books on your bookshelf.

- The magazines you read.
- The websites you visit.
- The shows you watch.
- Etc.

You probably already spend a lot of your time reading, watching and consuming all kinds of material related to what you like, and it would be a great topic for your own book.

Do you love running and own every copy of *Runner's World*? You could write a book compiling all the best tips and diet tricks for people who want to start running.

Do you, like my mother, watch every reality show about refurbishing, decorating, renting or selling houses? (And when I say she watches all of them, I mean ALL). You could write a book about how to decorate your house on a shoestring to increase its value.

The best part of this strategy is that you'll enjoy doing the research for your book as you'll be learning more about something you're already passionate about.

4. What things others are interested in.

(Benefits)

If there's nothing people tend to ask you about, you haven't overcome any obstacles to write home about, and you don't have an interest in any particular subject (which would surprise me), there's still no need to worry. You can write about other people's interests.

This has a big advantage when it comes to selling your book (not so much when it comes to writing it in the first place), because you're writing about a topic that you already know people are prepared to pay to read about.

So how do you know what these topics are?

a) Amazon categories and subcategories.

Go to the book department on Amazon and start navigating through the menu on the left. There, you'll find subcategories you had no idea existed. If there is a considerable number of books on a certain topic in Amazon's categories, you can bet your ass that there's an audience for it, no matter how weird you might personally find it.

b) Published magazines.

The editorial business side of magazine publishing lives off companies paying to have ads within their pages. The way to convince these companies to hire their services is to show them there is a large segment of the population interested in their subject - so, going down to the newsagent and taking a look at their magazine selection is a great way to get ideas on what to write about in order to have guaranteed potential customers.

c) Online courses on Udemy, Skillshare, etc.

More and more people, when deciding to learn something new, opt for online courses - especially on platforms like Udemy, which offer great courses for less than the price of a book. This means the variety and quality of these courses is getting bigger all the time, and these platforms are an amazing place to find ideas for your book.

Brainstorming

Now that you know four different strategies for finding a good idea for your book, it's time to get to it. All you need to do is set aside fifteen to thirty minutes in your diary to sit down with a pen and paper.

During this time, write as many ideas as you can for each of the four strategies we just looked at. I'm sure that some will produce more ideas than others, but try to write down at least five for each one.

It's important to use a pen and paper for this part, rather than a laptop or phone (and this is coming from a compulsive techie). The process of writing by hand engages a different part of your brain, which can help you to have even more ideas.

How to choose which book to write first

While some people may find it hard to come across a good idea they can turn into a book, others might have the opposite problem. It sounds like a great problem to have, but it can lead to what is known as "analysis paralysis".

If this sounds like you, ask yourself the following:

- Which idea would you most like to write about?
- Which book do you think will sell the most?
- Which book can you finish fastest?

I ask myself these three questions both when it comes to writing a book and when I'm creating a new project (in the latter case, I also ask myself "which requires the least investment?").

Depending on the situation you're in, some of these points are more valid than others. If, for example, you've just found yourself out of a job and you need some income to cover your basic needs, you should, of course, focus on the book that will sell the most copies.

It may be that all your needs are covered and what you're looking for is self-actualization through sharing something you're passionate about with the world. Or maybe you've taken a little time off work and your priority is to finish the book as fast as possible before you go back to work.

Given that each question carries weight, it can help to use a table:

	Book 1	Book 2	Book 3	...
What idea would you most like to write about?				
What book do you think would sell the best?				
What book could you finish most quickly?				

Assign a value from 1 to 3 to each question and each book. Once you've finished, add up the values and you'll get a book view of which book you should start with.

If you're in a place where some questions carry more weight than others, like in the examples I gave, then double your value for them - 2, 4, or 6, instead of 1, 2, or 3.

If you've done the exercise and still don't know which book to write, don't worry. Take a few days' break and come back to it. Remember that many budding writers have to do this exercise multiple times before their brainwave finally happens.

And finally... Don't get stressed.

Even if you spend a month or two writing a book that doesn't hit the *New York Times* bestseller list, you will still:

- Have an asset that can generate recurrent passive income for you.
- Have learned a lot about the book-writing process.
- Have much more confidence when it comes to starting a new book.

So, once you've done the exercise at least a couple of times, choose the book that feels right for you *now*. You can always come back and do it again later, with some more learning under your belt.

The title: secret to success nº1

You might think that writing a great book —a book people love— guarantees your success. Well, I'm sorry to say this isn't always the case - especially if you're an unknown writer.

Did you know that the first novel of Joanne Rowling, the creator of Harry Potter, was rejected by twelve publishing houses before eventually turning her into the first female writer in history to become a billionaire? Do you know how much Joanne earned from her book from the time she wrote it to when it finally fell into her readers hands, five years later? That's right...nothing!

Clearly, having a book people love and a book people buy are NOT the same thing. To earn money from your book, whether it's good or not so much, you have to reach your readers first.

Until now, whether or not your book reaches potential readers depended on a stupid publishing house deciding that your book was worthy of being published - and believe me, there are plenty of stupid publishing houses (like the twelve idiots that rejected Harry Potter). It's just like the stupid banks who laughed in the faces of Steve Jobs or Amazon's Jeff Bezos over forty times.

Luckily for you, nowadays, you don't need a publishing house to help you reach your readers and decide your book is worthy - *all you have to do is upload your book to Amazon and let them promote it for you!*

Unlike going through a traditional publishing house, this does not require any ass-kissing; no one has to like you, nor do you have to be lucky enough for that one specific person to like your book (someone who might be embittered by their own writing failures, or just plain having a bad day).

For Amazon to promote your book, all you have to do is do things right. And this starts with **your book's title.** It doesn't matter how well-written your book is or its ability to change lives and revolutionize the world - if Amazon doesn't show it to its potential readers, that's the end of the story. Period. Finito.

5 keys for winning over Amazon (and your readers) with the title of your book.

1. Keep an eye on the competition.

What better place to start than the titles of your competition? I can say from experience that most of the titles you'll see can be classified in one of the following three ways:

1. **100% SEO[7]-oriented**. You want search engines to favor you and put you in key positions, but don't forget you're writing for people, not just algorithms.

2. **Excessively creative**. Grabbing people's attention is important, but it's also important that when somcone reads the title of your book, they know what the hell it's about!

3. **Boring**. Many authors decide on their books' titles while trying not to stand out too much, thinking that will help them

---

[7] SEO stands for search engine optimization, which is a set of practices designed to improve the appearance and positioning of web pages in organic search results.

reach as many people as possible. What they don't realize is that **if you're writing for everybody, you're not writing for anybody.**

The aim of keeping an eye on the competition is to give you an idea of the general tone of books in your field and **avoid making the same mistakes they have**. Of course, well-known writers can afford to use both hugely boring and excessively creative titles and still sell thousands of copies - but you and I have to do our homework.

2. Minimum viable SEO.

There is no faster or more effective way to ensure your book will be shown to your potential clients than by using keywords - or SEO techniques - in its title. Why is it so important to use keywords?

- Keywords determine your book's positioning on Amazon.

- Keywords determine your book's ranking on Google.
- Keywords determine how many Amazon pages your book will appear on - for example, "customers also bought…".

Of all the keywords in your book, the most important ones are in the title. Don't worry - to have a good SEO strategy, all you need to do is follow these simple steps:

- Google the phrase "*Google Keyword Planner*" and select the first result that appears.
- Click "Go to Keyword Planner".
- If you don't have an account, you'll need to create one by going to "New *Google Ads* Account" (don't worry, it's free).
- Click "Discover new keywords", write down all the words and phrases that come to mind related to your topic, and click "Get results".

- Click on "Average monthly searches". This will organize your results by search volume.
- Choose between ten and fifteen results that have at least a thousand searches a month and that could be used as a basis for your book title. Choose ones with *low* competition or, at the very least, *medium.*

Now that you have your list of keywords, you can move on to the next part.

3. Hit the sore points.

We open our wallets unthinkingly in order to relieve a current sore point (those extra pounds, a relationship break-up, and so on). But we think about it much more when it's about relieving a future sore point. They sell more aspirin than vitamins, put it that way.

Your title should focus on the main sore points your book can resolve for your readers: what can it do for them, and why should they be interested? First, find out your target audience's main sore point, and then create a title that tells them you can relieve it.

4. Show your personality.

If you've read my book *Branding Secrets*, you'll know I place a lot of stock in the idea of "brand differentiation". This term is rooted in the notion that it's more important (and lucrative) to be **different** than to be **better**.

Don't be afraid to show your personality: it's a hugely potent weapon that will enable you to differentiate yourself and stand out from the competition. Let me give you an example:

a) 100% SEO title: How to write a book: writing and publishing a book on Amazon.

b) SEO + Personality: How to write and publish a book on Amazon for people who hate writing.

You might think the latter title is risky. Many people believe that if you hate writing, you're not a real writer or that you should find other work. You might be thinking this title could cost you a lot of potential customers. But I'll say it again (I had to hear it several times before I finally got it):

If you're writing for everybody, you're not writing for anybody.

5. Include a time frame.

Now you have a title with all the elements necessary to win Amazon around, thanks to the minimum viable SEO you've applied, hitting your readers' sore points, and standing out from the competition with a splash of personality.

Your potential client is now clear on what they can expect from your book - all that's left is to tell them when they will get that result. We live in a here-and-now society, so it's inevitable that your prospective customer will wonder when they can expect to see the promised benefits. Why not answer their question before they've even asked it?

There are myriad expressions you can use: "in less than an hour", "in 30 days"...Just be careful not to create unrealistic expectations.

Now that we've gone through everything, you can put it all together and apply the following, **Formula for the Perfect Title**:

FPT = keywords (SEO) + solution (sore point) + personality + time frame.

Bear in mind that you won't always be able to or want to use each and every one of these elements. That's why I advise you to create at least two combinations and do a little poll among your friends and family to help you take a step back and have the best chances of success.

At this point, you have a good driving force to help you overcome any writers' block that might crop up along the way, you've hit upon the perfect idea for your (first) book, and you've created a super-title that inspires you and keeps you focused. **It's time to write.**

How to write your book

As I confessed earlier, I've always considered writing to be among my biggest weak points. The fact that it took my first book - at just over thirty thousand words long - four years to finish is proof of that. I could never have imagined that one day I would be writing books for a living - much less that I would be helping others to do the same.

Luckily, the day I decided I wanted to turn writing into a way of life (rather than a four-year torment for each book), I had a very powerful weapon, and one I consider to be my greatest superpower: LAZINESS.

I'm a very **persistent** person (or stubborn, whatever) and if I set out to do something, I find a way to do it. But I'm also **tremendously lazy**. The mix of these two opposing qualities has a wonderful result: I always find the easiest way to get what I want.

This efficient way of doing things is actually known as the **Pareto Principle** or **80/20 Rule**. It means that generally speaking, and for a wide range of phenomena, approximately **80% of consequences come from 20% of causes**.

- 80% of wealth is accumulated by 20% of the population.
- 80% of a hospital's resources are used by 20% of its patients.
- 80% of a company's revenue comes from 20% of its clients.
- 20% of the carpet in your house or office gets 80% of the foot traffic.
- Etc.

Applying this principle to the academic field enabled me to always be top of the class despite being one of the students who spent the least time studying, and in sports it allowed me to be one of the most "ripped" at the gym even though I worked out a fraction as much as the others.

What I mean by this is that spending less time on a task but doing it in the most efficient way won't give you worse results - quite the opposite. Focusing on the most important aspects of the task rather than trying to take on the whole thing will get you **better results with less effort**. We're going to apply this when it comes to writing your book.

To do this, I've developed a **simple 3-step** system: create a **mind map**, do a little **research** and draw up a **blueprint**.

1. The magic of mind maps.

For this first part, we're going to employ a tool widely used to extract information: mind maps.

When you complete this exercise, you'll realize that you have much more to write about than you could have possibly imagined. If you take it seriously and dedicate enough time to it, your book will virtually write itself.

Just like we did with your book's title, when it comes to creating a mind map, it helps to use a pen and paper to stimulate your creativity and give you more ideas than doing it digitally.

The first thing you have to do is write your title (the main idea) in the middle of your sheet of paper and then draw a circle around it. Now, it's time to juice your memory and creativity: start by making notes around the title of all the ideas that pop into your head relating to your book's topic, connecting to that inner circle by lines. Think about the different areas your book could discuss: examples, personal experiences, articles you've read or saved, movies...

As you note down these main ideas or themes, you'll think of new sub-themes related to them. Draw a new circle around the main ideas and note these subtopics around them just like you did with the book title, and so on and so forth. You can use colors, drawings, cuttings, and more.

Your mind map should start to look like this:

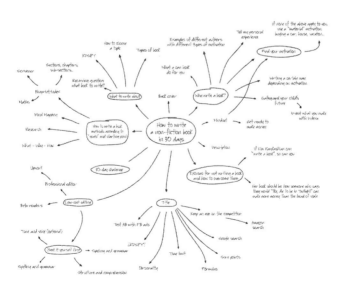

Keep drawing circles and lines to new ideas for as long as you can: fifteen minutes minimum. Set a timer if you have to.

If you run out of paper, don't hesitate to grab another sheet and keep expanding your mind map as much as you can. I've seen mind maps bigger than a king-size bed, so don't hold back.

There are two rules to bear in mind while you're completing this exercise:

1. No filters.

Don't limit your imagination; any idea that comes to mind is a valid one. Nothing is extraneous, nothing too crazy.

2. Leave perfectionism at the door.

If your mind map isn't a total mess...you're doing it wrong! Your mind map is NOT there to be framed and hung on a wall - it's for getting as many ideas out of your head as you can. If you try to make it look pretty or structured, you will be limiting your creativity. There will be time to shape it a little in the third step.

2. The power of research.

Now that you've squeezed the right side of your brain, it's time to put the more analytical left side to use. Now is the time to activate your investigative superpowers.

When it comes to the ESSENTIAL task of research, I've come across two types of writer:

a) **Those who love research** (or are mega-perfectionists, like me). They can spend months or even years (I'm proof) looking for every snippet of information on the subject they want to write about. Their books may never see the light of day.

b) **Those who skip research.** These authors find the research process so unbelievably tedious that they just go with their instincts and skip it altogether.

Striking a balance between too much and too little research is one of the challenges you'll face on the exciting journey to writing your book.

To finish your mind map with some important ideas or points you might have forgotten or not known about, and to **avoid falling into analysis paralysis during the research stage**, we're going to use Pareto's Principle, or 80/20 Rule that we looked at at the beginning of this chapter. The hardest part of applying this principle is working out which are the 20% of tasks with the potential to get 80% of the results.

I present to you: "the Holy Trinity of research for non-fiction writers".

- Kindle's content index.

- Amazon reviews.
- The top three books in your field (optional).

a) Kindle's content index.

Go on Amazon, look for the ten highest-selling books in your book's category or field, and click "Look inside".

Once you're in, all you have to do is go to the index or contents page. Within the *Holy Trinity* of research for non-fiction writers, this is, without a doubt, the Holy Grail.

Where to find the "Look inside" button.

As well as noting down on your mind map any new ideas you come across while looking through the contents of these ten bestsellers, this point will also enable you to see:

- The number of sections, chapters and subchapters that tend to be necessary for your book's topic.
- Which chapters/ideas are included across all the books.
- Which chapters/ideas are NOT included in all of them. Maybe your book doesn't need them either (we'll find that out in the next point: Amazon reviews).
- How many pages (or words) tend to be devoted to each aspect.

Note: Just because you're noting down new ideas from these contents tables in your mind map, doesn't mean you have to write about them in your book. You can decide that later, and it will depend on your strategy.

b) Amazon reviews.

This method of research will enable you to go from a "complete" book to a book people actually love. What's more, unlike the contents page method, almost nobody does this.

If you do your homework right, discarding boring or generic reviews ("I love this book", "I hate this book", "This book didn't arrive on time", and the like) and focus on the specific, detailed reviews, you can figure out:

- **What points your readers felt were lacking**. If you find several readers complaining that a certain type of information was missing from all or most of the books on your chosen topic, you've stumbled upon a gold mine: take advantage of it to differentiate yourself and stand out from the competition.
- **What points you can skip**. Maybe you can skip over excessively basic aspects or

omit any that are overly technical. Always keep in mind the audience you're writing for. Don't try to tackle everything. Less is more.

- **What aspects readers truly grasped**. Maybe it's the books' clarity or structure, maybe it's the use of examples, maybe it's that they felt they could relate to the writer. Pay attention and take note.

- **What aspects readers were annoyed by**. It may be something as simple as correcting grammar mistakes or not generating unrealistic expectations with the books' titles. Try to avoid those pitfalls.

c) The three best books in your field (optional).

If you're thinking about writing a book, you've probably already read the top titles in your chosen field - if you haven't, I strongly recommend that you do. You probably won't find any ideas beyond what you found in their indexes or reviews (although you might), but you need to know who you're up against. It's not that you're going to copy them or try to go one better, but you do need to get an idea of **what made these books nº 1** and, above all, **how you can stand out**.

If your mind map was already kind of tangled before you even began your research process, it will probably be total chaos by the time you finish it. Don't worry; that's pretty normal. It's time to give method to the madness.

Pro tip: this is somewhat optional, but once I've "finished" writing up my mind map, I spend half an hour typing it up on an online app like _MindNode_[8] (available for cellphone and PC). This means that when I get a new idea, I can easily add it to the map. Carrying a king-size version around with you isn't awfully practical.

---

[8] soykevinalbert.com/mindmap

IMPORTANT! Not taking enough of an interest in creating this mind map can lead you to spend hours upon hours sitting in front of a blank page, banging your head against the wall trying to think of what the hell you're going to write.

Failing to create a mind map will probably lead to failing to create your book. Don't make that mistake.

3. Blueprint structure.

Once you've sampled the magic of mind maps and added your *minimum viable research*, it's time to give the magic some structure. We're going to turn your chaotic mind map into a structured, easy-to-follow blueprint that will serve as your GPS.

Just like how your GPS will stop you from having to slam the brakes on your car every time you reach an intersection or have to lean out the window to ask someone which road leads to Rome (I promise that when it comes to writing a book, not all of them will), the blueprint for your book will help you to relax along the way and enjoy the writing journey.

To turn your mind map into a good GPS (not one of those that yell "turn!" when you're halfway down the highway), we're going to put it through three simple checks.

Check 1: Find the sections, chapters and subchapters.

The first thing you need to do is take a step back and gain some perspective. Don't let yourself not see the wood for the trees. Are you able to distinguish the main topics or sections into which you'll divide your book?

Grab a fresh sheet of paper and write these sections at the top, as headings. Once you've done this, I want you to put the rest of your ideas (all of them) under the section they fit best with. If you find that an idea fits into more than one section, add it to both and connect them with arrows.

Once you've written all your ideas in, draw a circle around those that can be used as chapters in your book, and join them with lines to the subchapters or main points to talk about for each.

Your blueprint will start to look like this:

Don't be afraid to leave ideas out; we're in the middle of the distillation process, and this is what's supposed to happen. If your book can do without elements that are either very basic or very advanced, don't hesitate to cross them off. You don't have to create the most advanced book on a given topic; you just have to create a book that's different from others on your chosen subject.

Remember: Different is better than better.

Note: if your book is not very long, you may not need to create sections; the headings for this initial blueprint can be the chapters themselves.

Check 2: Digitalize your blueprint in a logical sequence.

Once you've identified your sections, chapters and subchapters, it's time to move from paper to computer. All you have to do while digitalizing your blueprint is order all of these points in a logical sequence that will allow readers to easily follow your book's flow. Start with the sections, then complete them by adding chapters and, finally, subchapters.

You may need to go beyond these subchapters and incorporate points and sub-points. Go into as much depth as necessary. These points and sub-points don't need to be included in your book's contents page, but they will help you when it comes to writing.

Check 3: Do the math.

It's time for our final check, which will result in your "definitive" blueprint/index which you will use to begin working on your book. For this last check, you're going to need a calculator.

Have you already thought about how many pages you want your book to have? If not, now is the time to do it. You can use your favorite books as a benchmark or refer to the bestsellers in your field (the ones you researched in the previous stage). Now, I'm going to explain why.

Let's say you want to write a thirty-thousand-word book. Now, divide this number into the number of chapters in your blueprint. This calculation will tell you how many words each chapter needs to contain.

Why do these numbers matter?

- Once you know how many words you can write per hour, you'll know how long you should dedicate each day to your book in order to finish in the time you've set yourself.
- You can reorganize all your chapters - joining some together and splitting others - if you see that there's a big imbalance between them.
- A very low number of words per chapter may indicate that it could be a good idea to divide your book into multiple books. This

is a good time to do it: creating two or more blueprints based on your original blueprint. Sometimes, each section can make a great book all on its own.

If you've followed all the directions in this chapter, by now you should have an invaluable blueprint in your hands and be ready to begin your 'writer in 30 days' challenge.

If you decided to give this chapter - or the whole book - a re-read first, before starting to write (which I think is a great idea), I really want to hammer home the importance of not skipping this point. If you don't take the time to complete the steps we've looked at so far, writing your book could be a real nightmare. Preparing a good blueprint for your book might take a few hours or even days. but it will save you months or years of work down the line. Please, don't try to take a shortcut here: your blueprint *is* the shortcut. I promise you'll thank me later.

Challenge: Writer in 30 days

Once you've finished your blueprint, it's time to start writing your book. In this chapter, I'm going to show you how to finish your book's first draft in 30 days or less.

To sign up for this challenge, all you have to do is commit to following two simple steps:

1. You can't start editing until you reach the end of your book.
2. You can't take on any other projects during these 30 days.

Do you accept the challenge?

Fuckeable Tournament: The birth of the "writer in 30 days" challenge.

As I've mentioned several times in this book, one of my many facets is as a personal trainer. But not just some guy who says he's a personal trainer: a real one, with certifications and everything!

With over twenty years' experience, having worked with hundreds of clients (both pro and amateur), and, above all, having applied the 80/20 Rule to my working methodology, I was able to start guaranteeing results many years ago.

Before I start work with a client, we set some objectives - usually yearly ones - and if we don't reach them, I give the customer his or her money back (ALL of it). To date, I've never had to refund any of my clients. Obviously, this is because I have a great work system... but it's also because I keep an ace up my sleeve: **challenges and contests**.

No matter how well you do things, in the world of fitness you can (and will) experience plateaus or blocks where you stop progressing for a few weeks or even months. This is pretty normal, and it's often resolved by just being patient. But, since I guarantee results and losing a year's pay leaves kind of a bitter taste, when a client reaches this point I organize a mini contest or tournament lasting a month or two.

During these tournaments, workouts don't get longer or more intense, nor do diets get stricter. But they **always** help people overcome plateaus and blockages, and sometimes even allow for more progress than the entire year prior. How is this possible?

1. **Short-term aims**. Long-term goals are, without a doubt, the most important kind - but distance in time can mean these aims lose their ability to motivate. A short-term aim is easier to measure and visualize, which amplifies its power.

2. **Intrinsic motivation**. A competitive setting involves an element of challenge that gives participants the chance to compare their skills with those of other competitors and assess their own achievements. This is why I always find another client who wants to take part, or - "worst" case scenario - they compete against me as their coach.

3. **Extrinsic motivation**. The winner, in addition to the reward inherent to having improved their appearance in record time, wins a prize agreed upon by participants in advance. Sometimes, we even throw in punishments, too :)

4. **Peer "pressure" or support**. One thing I ask of my clients during these competitions is that they post their goal on social media. When you share your objectives with people around you, it

makes them more real. Feeling that people are watching your progress makes you more committed, and - of course - they'll often cheer you on, too.

So much progress can be made with these kinds of challenges that, a few years ago, I started to use them myself, and created the *Fuckeable Tournaments:* contests developed to compete against my friends and give us an extra push toward that summer body.

As I'm sure you can understand, I can't show you the tournaments of my private customers...but you can see the ones with my friends. I made it a condition of taking part that they let me share their photos ;)

Don't be scared → *www.fuckeable.com*

Seeing the potential of these challenges, I decided to design the "Writer in 30 days" challenge. It applies the same principles and very similar methodology to the fitness tournaments, and it gets the same extraordinary results in record time. As it happens, I'm writing this book right now using the very same system, and competing against my girlfriend and a friend of ours.

Impatient to find out exactly what this challenge consists of?

Writer in 30 days: The challenge.

Just like with my fitness challenges, the *Writer in 30 days* challenge helps turn a generally hard process into a stimulating journey that can even be fun.

To help you understand and follow it more easily, I've divided the challenge into 3 fundamental parts: planning, organization, and competition.

1. Planning.

a) Set a final objective.

You need to start with the end in mind. The first step will be to determine your final goal for this challenge: **to finish the first draft of your book within 30 days**.

Since you have already done your research by now and know, among other things, how many chapters your book will have and roughly how many words you want to write in total, you can now go into more depth.

Your final aim could be: **to write X number of chapters** (the total number set out in your blueprint) in 30 days or **to write X number of words** (the total number in your book) in 30 days.

b) Set a daily objective.

Let's say you want to write a 30,000-word book with 10 chapters within 30 days. The next step will be to divide this final objective into daily ones - so, divide it by 30. This means your daily goal will be to write a chapter every 3 days, or 1000 words a day.

Knowing how much you need to write each day will give you accurate insight into your progress and tell you whether or not you can achieve your goal within the specified timeframe.

c) Set weekly goals.

You may not feel like spending the same amount of time writing your book every day; some days you'll be more motivated and write much more than your daily goal, and some you'll barely be able to churn out a few words. This is why it's important to set intermediate goals or milestones.

For this challenge, it's best to divide the final goal into four and review them each week. Following the previous example, your weekly aim would be to write two and a half chapters, or 7,500 words.

4. Organization.

a) Draw up a writing timetable.

The best way to progress with your book is to plan your day in advance and schedule specific blocks of time during which you can totally focus on writing - if possible, always in the same place and at the same time. Remember, we're trying to create a routine that makes things easier for you. If you wait for free time to just pop up during the day so that you can write, you'll NEVER finish your book.

I recommend setting aside at least an hour a day. If you have more time some days and you feel inspired, keep going for as long as your schedule allows, or until your inspiration runs dry. Of course, this will depend a lot on the length of your book and on how many words you can write in an hour. When you get to the end of the first week, review your weekly goal for week 1, and adjust as needed.

Not sure how you're going to find the time? Well, I have a lot of ideas: try getting up a half hour earlier, going to bed an hour later, cutting down on TV time, social media or other leisure, skip the gym or evening classes for a month, and so on. Obviously, this will all depend on how motivated you are and how important writing your book is to you, but it's essential that you schedule your time blocks in advance.

If possible, try to write when you're most productive: the times at which you feel freshest and most creative. For some people, this is first thing in the morning after their coffee; others feel more inspired right before bed; others when they wake up from an afternoon nap, and so on. Decide what the best time is for you and try to stick to it every day.

Do the same with the place you write in. Do you focus better at home? Prefer to go to the library? Could you maybe write at the beach or a peaceful park?

Personally, I write at around ten o'clock in the morning - it takes me a while to fully wake up - at some charming little cafe or other, accompanied by my laptop and notebook. Whenever I try to do it at a different time or in a different place, my productivity suffers a lot.

b) Switch off.

In the digital age we're living in, we are always connected. Many people (including myself) feel a compulsive need to check their social media or emails on their phones. I get annoyed just seeing the badge on an app to tell me I have unread messages (it's an OCD thing for me).

These distractions can seriously damage your productivity and present a great obstacle in your writing routine. This is why it's hugely important that you switch off from everything when you sit down to write, especially if you're easily distracted.

Turn off your phone and disconnect your laptop from the wifi: two essential steps when it comes to beginning your routine. Do what it takes to ensure that the only thing you can focus on during this time is your book, and nothing else.

c) Your author routine.

Now that you know how much you need to write each day and you've scheduled your time blocks, let's look at exactly what your daily routine as an author will consist of.

Remember why you're doing this (1 min). It's as simple as it sounds. Before you start writing, remember why you decided to write this book, and jot it down. This simple exercise will help to refocus you and get you through the difficult days.

Mind map for each chapter (15 min). Every time you start a new chapter, you're going to create a miniature mind map for that specific chapter.

Grab a blank sheet of paper, write the chapter's title in the center, and draw a circle around it. Now, just like you did with your overall blueprint, draw lines coming off of this and note down any ideas you have relating to that chapter: points, sub-points, examples, stories, and so on.

Fill out your blueprint (5 min). Once you've finished this mini mind map, go back to your overall blueprint and add any new ideas you just had for that chapter.

WRITE (40-90 min). Using your blueprint as a GPS, start your timer and write for as long as you said you would. Since you already know what you're going to talk about and the sequence you'll do it in, the writing process shouldn't hold any surprises. So get scribbling!

In short, your daily routine should look like this:

1. **Why**: 1 minute.
2. **Mind map**: 15 minutes (only on days when you start a new chapter).
3. **Blueprint**: 5 minutes (as above).
4. **Write**: 40-90 minutes.

5. Competition.

a) Find your competitors.

Competing against yourself is fine. Setting daily and weekly goals to fulfil will help you get through and finish your book in the allotted time. But you can't deny that **it's fun to compete against other people, as well as highly motivational**.

One of the most important factors for a writer - especially a first-time one - to be successful (ie to finish their book) is third party supervision. I'm sure you've seen movies where the star, a successful author, experiences writers' block and would be tempted to take a year's sabbatical if not for their editor on their back day and night. Of course, he ends up meeting his deadline, his publisher renews his contract, he gets the girl and lives happily ever after.

Well, that is exactly what your competitor or competitors are going to do with you, only less annoyingly. All you need to do is schedule a couple of sessions (face-to-face or over videocall) where you can share your aims and daily or weekly progress. This will activate your competitive streak, and you'll be spurred on to keep getting better. *"If they can do it, what's stopping me?"*

In these sessions, not only do you share your goals and progress (not the same thing) with each other, but also your best practice, any difficulties you encounter along the way, tricks you've picked up, and anything you think could contribute to your own success and that of your rivals.

With the *Fuckeable* Tournaments, we don't even need to schedule these mini-sessions. Our progress - measured in weight and body fat - is recorded automatically in the cloud, since we all own the same smart scale. We all have access to each other's data. As well as this, we monitor calories in and distance walked (through the same app), which helps give us an idea of why progress is or isn't happening, and either copy other participants or help them out.

Note: If you don't know anyone in the same position as you who you could compete against, try to find someone you trust who can check on your progress every day or week.

b) Broadcast your goal to the world.

As well as sharing your goals and progress with your fellow competitors, I recommend that you share them publicly on your social media and with family and friends.

This will add some extra commitment. Deciding to do something, keeping it to yourself, and then changing your mind is no big deal - but it's another thing entirely to know you're going to have to explain to dozens of people that you threw in the towel on that objective you claimed was so important to you.

This will also garner you additional support - sometimes, from unexpected people. Maybe one of your colleagues has written a book too, and would love to follow your progress and help you along the way.

Finally, shouting it from the rooftops is an amazing (and sneaky) way to promote your book. People who get involved and follow your progress will feel like part of the project, and they'll want to buy your book when it comes out.

c) Celebrate your wins.

Getting into the habit of celebrating your achievements and wins - no matter how small - can be very powerful when it comes to accomplishing your present and future objectives.

If you've found an opponent or group of opponents to compete against, then during the first mini-session you schedule together, agree upon a prize for the winner or winner.

If you took a look at the *Fuckeable Tournaments*, you will have seen that we have an individual prize (affordable) as well as collective prizes, like a "cheat meal" together or photoshoot to immortalize our beach bodies.

If you haven't managed to find anyone to compete against, before you write a single word, decide how you're going to celebrate on day 30, when you've finished your book. Writing a book is something millions of people dream about, but only a select group of fighters ever make it. Don't undervalue what you've achieved; reward yourself like you deserve.

Once you've celebrated having finished your first draft, **it's time to edit your book.**

Low-cost editing

I know: you've just undertaken the mammoth task of writing your book (something 99% of people want to do but never will), and in record time! I know the last thing you want to do is start checking it over and correcting it, so I have good news for you: the first step in the editing process is REST. **And it's not optional**.

Celebrate having finished your book, and let a week go by. Then, it's time to dust off that draft and start sculpting it into a true work of art.

Spoiler alert: the first time you re-read your draft, it's going to seem nothing like a work of art.

During the editing process, your book will pass through three sets of hands: yours, your beta readers', and a professional editor's.

Phase 1: self-editing.

The first check needs to be done by you, and it's going to be a triple check. This means that rather than reading your book through once and trying to correct it all in one go, you're going to read it three times, paying attention to a specific aspect each time. If you try to fix it all in one go, you'll find it an uphill struggle and you'll feel like you've stalled (which you may well have done).

1. On your **first check**, all you're allowed to do is **underline and take notes** of the errors and inconsistencies you come

across, in addition to any improvements you'd like to make.

2. On the **second**, you should pay attention to the **coherence and fluidity** of your text: reorganize sections or even add and take away from them as needed.

3. On your **third and final check**, all that's left is to go through your **spelling and grammar** mistakes.

That's it: your book is ready to move onto the next phase. Don't keep checking it over forever. This is one of the biggest mistakes an author can make. It's better to have a finished imperfect book than one "perfect" chapter in an unfinished book.

Don't forget: "Finished is better than perfect".

Phase 2: beta readers.

If two heads are better than one, imagine what twenty can see. Beta readers are an amazing way to get feedback during your book's editing process: finding inconsistencies and grammatical errors, giving you an idea of how your book will be received by future readers, and more.

A beta reader is basically anyone who reads your book's draft and offers you constructive feedback (beyond just "I liked it" or "I didn't like it"). Your will benefit from their corrections and suggestions, and they will get a free copy of your draft.

Your close friends and family members aren't the best beta readers, since it's hard for them to be objective; they will be trying not to hurt your feelings. That's not what you need right now.

So where can you find your beta readers? Firstly, ask around the people who have been following your book's progress during the Writer in 30 days challenge and who are interested or knowledgeable about the topic of your book.

If none or very few of your "followers" meet these requirements, you can find beta readers in Facebook groups around your topic or general non-fiction reading.

Once you've selected your beta readers, make sure that along with a digital copy of your draft, you send them some basic indications of what you're expecting from them. It could be simply underlining any grammatical errors they encounter while reading, or a short list of specific questions on the content of your book.

What should you look for in the feedback you receive? You don't have to go with every single suggestion from your beta readers when modifying your book. You can't please everyone, and trying is a big mistake. What you're looking for are common points. Find the suggestions that come up over and over and decide if you need to make some last-minute modifications before moving onto the third phase.

Phase 3: your professional editor.

We're almost there. We've made it to the third and final phase of editing your book and we're about to turn that chaotic draft you started checking just a few days ago into a real masterpiece.

Your book has now been through three self-checks by you and one by your beta readers, so you might be tempted to skip this last step and save a few bucks. Don't make that mistake.

Your checks and those of your beta readers have certain limitations. Having a professional editor go into depth on your work is **a very important step before you click "publish".**

A good editor can help you polish your draft, fix any small (or not so small) faux pas, and offer you suggestions on how to improve your book. It's easy to find a professional editor, but getting it cheap is less easy. Fortunately, I wrote a whole book on precisely this.

Of all the places where you can find an editor for your book, I recommend _Upwork_[9], a virtual marketplace that puts the best freelancers from all over the world in touch with companies or individuals looking for talented professionals.

Basically, all you have to do is sign up to the platform and post your job offer (editing your book) following the steps the site tells you to. You'll start getting proposals from dozens of freelancers interested in editing your book. Your only task is to find the professional offering the best quality for the best price.

---

[9] upwork.com

How to choose your editor

The best thing about working with a platform like Upwork is that you can check the profiles of all the freelancers offering to edit your book: their rates, training, portfolios, and, above all, their reviews.

You could get lost in all the information on show and spend days reading profiles. But you don't need to. Here's how I do it:

First, I discard proposals from any freelancers who have earned less than $12,000 on the platform or who have a client satisfaction rating of under 90%. Already, this will reduce your shortlist to just a few offers. Among the professionals still standing, take a look to see if any of them specialize in, or have background in, your book's topic. Mark them as your favorites.

All that's left to do now is discuss prices.

How much does it cost to edit a book with Upwork?

The answer is simple: however much you want to spend.

For years now, I've used Upwork for one thing or another almost every week (you can't imagine the scope of the things you can commission there). The first thing I learned about working with these platforms is that, just like in the offline world, prices vary *to infinity and beyond*.

For the same book (thirty thousand words, let's say), two freelancers with the same degree of training and experience might charge you a hundred dollars or over five thousand.

Official prices for editing a book are generally considered to be between $0.005 and $0.015 per word, as recommended by the Editorial Freelancers Association. But that doesn't mean you won't find rates far higher or lower with similar results. This abysmal difference depends on various factors, the main one being the freelancer's country of origin, since it's more expensive to live in the US than in, say, Thailand. But it can also depend on how in-demand or "famous" the freelancer is.

But don't be disheartened; this is the beauty of these marketplaces. Remember: if a professional has 90% client satisfaction or higher and has earned at least $12,000 on the platform, it's almost guaranteed that they will do a good job.

To help give you an idea, for my last few books (of between fifteen and thirty thousand words each), I paid on average $95.

And there you have it!

If your book has been through the three phases of editing (self-editing, beta readers and professional editing), you've finished your book.

CONGRATULATIONS! You did it!

If you're a super-perfectionist like me and you're tempted to keep checking your book over and over again, unnecessarily delaying its launch (just in case you find something you can improve on or some grammatical mistake to correct), remember: Amazon lets you keep making modifications to your book FOREVER, even after it's been published!

So, there's no excuse. If you followed all the steps in this book, I'm sure you have a masterpiece on your hands, and it deserves to see the light of day. Don't deprive the world of this privilege, and don't deprive yourself of the satisfaction.

It's time to publish your book.

What else is there to say?

At this point, all that's left is to congratulate you:

a) If this is the first time you've read this book and you're ready for action, well done! Of all the people who talk about writing a book, you're now part of that little 1% who actually do something and decide to educate themselves on how to make that dream come true.

In this book, you've learned:

- **How to figure out why you're doing it**. A sufficiently motivational reason that you don't have to depend on willpower or stubbornness.

- **How to overcome writers' block**. Now you know the obstacles that might crop up along the way, and how to beat them.
- **How to find the perfect idea for your book**, even if you thought you already had one.
- **How to create the perfect title**, one that Amazon will like and that will get you sales.
- **How to write your book in 30 days**. I've given you the exact system that enabled me to go from one book in four years to one book in under a month.
- **How to get your books edited on a budget**. Now you know how to get professional editing for amateur prices.

b) And, of course, if you've written your book by now, congratulations! You can proudly say **you're officially a writer.**

This is a real milestone in life, and one worth raising a glass to. I would love to be there with you to drink to it. Maybe one day, we'll meet and have that toast - but in the meantime, please do write and tell me about it. You can do this directly to my email at _books@soykevinalbert.com_, or even better, tell me in your Amazon review. I'd be very grateful. Oh! And you have my blessing to name drop your book there :)

So now what?

You've taken the most difficult step in every writer's journey: you have written your book.

Now: **publish it!**

- Is it better to go through a publishing house, or self-publish? What are the pros and cons of each?
- How can you avoid getting scammed by publishers?
- Can you self-publish with the same quality as with a publisher and with greater chances of success?
- What steps do you need to follow to upload a book to Amazon?

- Is it better to focus on Amazon or to have your book on lots of platforms?
- How do you set a price for your book? What do you need to bear in mind?

You'll find the answers to all these questions - and many more - in the second instalment: ***Successful Self-Publishing: How to publish a book without a (bloodsucking) publisher***.

Get yours now

soykevinalbert.com/ssp2

Don't let years go by before your book sees the light of day just because you're waiting for approval from a publishing house, and don't just self-publish without doing things properly and risk nobody buying your book.

Important

Like all my books, this is a beta version - that means that, just like me (I'm a beta male, after all), it will keep improving over time and with experience. For this to happen, **your opinion is essential**.

Please, leave me an Amazon review and let me know what you thought. What did you like best? Was there anything missing? Would you add anything, or take anything away?

Scan and leave a review

If, for some reason, you thought my book was a pile of trash, please email me and I will give you back 100% of your money for having wasted your time, and/or I will resolve any doubts you might still have.

The main factor that drives me to keep writing is helping people, so if I'm not doing that, I'll happily do something else instead.

Best of luck, fellow writer!
Kevin Albert

Manufactured by Amazon.ca
Bolton, ON

28447802R00085